# MARK REIF

# Vermont Winter Reflections

# Preface

The Vermont winter has many moods and visuals. They were especially apparent during my first winter in the state. I hope that with every line, you can feel each powder turn and take in the winter magic.

Mark Reif

# 1

# December 21, 2021

You're finally here
Arctic wind and bluish-white peaks
Smoky mists washing over the slopes
Now, morning time is a biting experience
The shock of cold air like mint in the atmosphere.

The tundra atop Mansfield
Was awash in the sunset
Beautiful, yet stark and rocky mountains
Speckles of white between the trees
As the frigid air blew and whistled

No more waiting for cold weather
It's here
And maybe even colder
As the days pass into January
The icy environment is a challenge
But the cost is worth the beauty

2

December 21, 2021

I begged and pleaded
For the cold weather to come
Now, I'm not so sure

With sharpened claws
Biting into my skin
The cold air has no sympathy
For human needs

Just a punching chill
Trying to work its way
Into every opening and crevice
Or take advantage
Of an open door

The frigid atmosphere
Hits you like a hammer
As you step outside
And try to survive

# 3

# December 25, 2021

Christmas in Vermont
I feel peace
I feel quiet
As if inside my own snow globe
The winter surroundings
Hug me like a down comforter

I think of the things I have
And feel thankful
I think of the things I want
And let negativity float away

My flannel shirt caresses my skin
And my senses calm further and further

I feel like I'm inside a cloud

# 4

## December 26, 2021

The cold wind doesn't care
It doesn't care where you've been
It doesn't care where you're going
It doesn't care who you are

The frigid, punishing wind
Just mindlessly blows against
Weathered rocks and frozen waterfalls
And it's up to you to survive it

You can't beg the wind to stop
You can't plead with it
Even when you hunker down
And cover yourself with your arms
It will not let up

The only upside to enduring
This tempest is
When you finally reach warm shelter

# 5

# December 30, 2021

Like a snowy owl
Perched high atop a tree
I ride high above the slopes
On the chairlift

Insulated from the cold
By my outerwear
The wind whips at me
And icicles hang off of rocks
Off on a mountain top

The day is drawing to a close
But I cruise around
On some mellow trails
My snowboard weaving around
Like a bicycle through city streets

The cold snow glides underneath my board
Glide, glide, glide, until I reach the village

6

# December 30, 2021

I waited for a while for the shuttle to arrive
After a long day of teaching snowboard lessons

My body worn down and
Needing a meal, I kept waiting
The driver promised he'd stop at the locker room
As more and more workers piled into the bus

Soon, it was apparent his route
Did not include my stop, so I began to trudge

Carrying my snowboard and outfitted
In heavy jacket and pants
I hiked past gridlocked traffic and across a parking lot
Reminiscent of a snowy desert

Finally, I reached the oasis
Where I could change, and return home

# 7

# December 30, 2021

On mornings like these
As dawn takes place
And I begin the drive to the mountain
I let go of the past
And embrace the present,
So thankful to experience this

My car is packed tight with my snowboard gear
And I'm dressed in an array
Of outerwear ready for
Cold snow, wind, and sun
And I love it

The sun rises over I-89
Then Route 100, then Mountain Road
I navigate the final turns before
The parking lot, before arriving
To shred up the slopes
Of Stowe Mountain Resort

8

# January 1, 2022

Snowboarding through the mountain fog
The whole world around goes quiet
As if I'm in a room full of pillows and blankets

Other skiers and snowboarders
Glide by and around my orbit
But all that matters
Is the snow beneath my board
Like soft, white tarmac

With each turn comes a swish
And snow sprays away
The steep slopes challenge me
And I work and work

As I reach the base of the mountain
I feel silence inside
All I perceive are the turns and the sensations
Until I reach the bottom and do it again

# 9

# January 3, 2022

Life is full of strain
And adjustments
Even getting through a regular day
Requires perseverance

But as I sit, absorbing the
Morning light through the windows,
Amplified by the snow on the tree branches,
I'm nourished by my surroundings,
Taking in their energy

I spend many hours alone
But I don't feel very alone
My friends and family are in
My orbit and I can think of them

And Vermont's countryside
And natural environment
Keep me company as time rolls by

# 10

## January 4, 2022

With each subsequent turn through the snow
I become shaped by the mountain
The wind whips at me
And fangs of ice hang from rocks

I'm alone on a white highway
Sometimes I'm exhilarated
Other times worn out and tired
But I cherish the experience
Of riding quality terrain

Instead of running 3–4 days a week
Now I ride 3–4 days a week
And it changes me inside and out

I await deep snows and big storms
But still, I'm pleased
With riding the snow
Already on the slopes

# 11

## January 6, 2022

Inside my personal snow globe
With the furnace blasting
And flurries falling outside the window
I take it all in, resting myself
After long days on the mountain

The snowflakes float and fly
Softly dropping to the ground
And the sturdy house
Traps the heat inside

On a soft couch, in cozy clothes
I rest and recover
Before once again
Venturing out into
The world of white

# January 6, 2022

Take in the stillness
Tired muscles relax and recover
Food cooks in the hot oven
Flakes fall gently in the night air

Vermont comes into its own
As winter takes hold
The snow lives happily
On the mountainsides
Safe from warmth until spring

The more snow that falls
The more the glades fill in
Exposing routes and runs
To take through the forest

Mt. Mansfield towers above
Standing over this winter scene

# 13

## January 8, 2022

At zero degrees
Things get serious

Daily worries and concerns
Fade away as you try to survive
Fingertips freeze and complain
Toes turn red with irritation

Even if you bundle up
As tightly as possible
The icy air will find a way in

My car starts with a lurch
Startled to be awoken
In such a harsh climate
And at such an early hour

My windshield's covered in ice
On the inside, further

Enhancing the struggle
To see the road ahead

The cold air
Will try to lull you to sleep
And allow you to give in
To stop running, or stop doing
Whatever it is you need to do

Hard and unforgiving
Like a slab of concrete
Zero-degree air dares you
To venture out into it

Then watches as you
Do your best to make it
Through the day

# 14

# January 11, 2022

I almost didn't go
I was worried about frostbite
Or some other type of danger
Almost like I was inside a spaceship
On a faraway planet

The subzero temperatures outside
Were a mystery to me
I hadn't yet felt them on my skin
Let alone go for a jog
And tax my system

But I thought it over for a while
And I ventured out the door
Bundled to the max
And with little exposed skin

The white, icy landscape
Was bright and still

And a powerful yellow sun
Shined downward

I ran like I always have
Stride after stride
But I felt the cold coming
Trying to catch me
In its grasp

About a mile out
I knew it was time to turn back
Frigid feelings were creeping
Inside of crevices
And my body needed the warm house

I made it back in one piece
Though it took a while to recover

Two or so miles felt
Like many more
But it was an interesting excursion

# 15

# January 15, 2022

The morning light nourishes me
The soft rays shine through the windows
Bringing energy back into my system
I relax and let troubles float away
Tension dissolves

Wearing my furry slippers
And enveloped by the velvet couch
I gaze at the surroundings
Of forest and snow
Largely untouched by modern society

Soon I will have to begin work
But I will meditate and savor
These fleeting moments
Before my consciousness
Returns to the real world

# 16

## January 15, 2022

The best mornings
Are when I am free
Responsibilities momentarily met
It's only me and the mountain

The sun rises up above the peaks
The arctic wind drives cold air
Up and over the terrain
And I revel in making turns on my snowboard

Forgetting how skillful I may be
I focus on soulful energy
Appreciating the feelings
Taking in the rustic forests

And concentrating
On the simple things
That make snowboarding
So wonderful

# 17

# January 15, 2022

When the subzero temps arrive
You could be living on another planet
The cold air burns exposed skin
Blood vacates extremities
And the human body attempts to adjust

We just weren't made for this
As though dropped from a spaceship
On a desolate orb
Where we hadn't evolved
The subzero air exposes our weaknesses

Once inside shelter
And saved by the warm air
Relief sets in
And the recovery begins

# 18

## January 17, 2022

The first big snow has arrived
I waited and waited
Sometimes disappointed
Other times wondering why
The winter had been so dry

But now the floodgates are open
And a relentless shower
Falls outside the window

Tree branches are weighed down
Covered in heaps of white
As the landscape changes
And green slowly disappears

I sit inside with my coffee
Patiently waiting for accumulations
So I can feel the fluff and plow down the mountain
On my snowboard

# 19

# January 20, 2022

Stowe trees and powder
Feel the glide
Ride the racetrack

Turn like a go-kart
Weave in and out
Soft pillows under your feet

Explore, then explore some more
No compass or map
Just feeling Mt. Mansfield
For all it's worth

Pivot right and left
Like a kid on a BMX bike
Feel the joy
Wearing yourself down
But keeping on going
Because it's just so much fun

# 20

# January 20, 2022

The vibrant sun through the windows
Gives me energy
Like a solar panel
I soak up its essence

Dark, cold days jar the body
But also weigh down your mood
Leaving you feeling like
An uncharged battery

Surviving winter in the
Frigid North requires effort
And fortitude beyond
More pleasant climates

A sunny day makes for a break
From the persistent cold
And subzero mornings
That test you each time

# 21

## January 21, 2022

Vermont sunset
Hold me tight
Put your hand in mine
Let's walk for a while

As you fade behind the trees
I feel your soft light
Outlines of branches
Painting silhouettes against the sky

Orange along the horizon
Fading into the blue sky
Before the world turns cold again
And the freeze begins

But just for this moment
Let's savor the twilight
And appreciate the natural world
Before tomorrow arrives

# 22

## January 21, 2022

The snow and ice crystals thrive
In the frigid air
While I endure
Under layers of clothing

The trees below the chairlift
Branches weighed down by snow
Happily exist above
The frozen surroundings

In some ways
Vermont is another world
Or maybe its own country
But it's entirely different

Cozy, harsh, eclectic, and pure
The landscape does what it wants
And welcomes those who adventure in
To experience its uniqueness

# 23

## January 26, 2022

When I removed my mittens
The skin began to freeze
I tried to move my fingers
But they stiffened and protested

Slowly, numbness took over
As feeling left my outer layer
Of human protection

The subzero air is not made
For humans thriving
It's a world of its own
White, blue, green and cold

I barely got the mittens back on
And my hands thanked me,
Gradually returning to normal
I rode the gondola
To the locker room

# 24

## January 26, 2022

The glide and feel
Of fresh snow under my snowboard
Is sweet relief from
Days gone by

I weave through the forest
Harvesting powder here and there
Looking for the next bounty
Hidden between logs and rocks

My turns are small and quick
Because I have to be
Like a nimble squirrel
Hunting for his sustenance

At the end, worn out
But exuberant and exhilarated
Stowe trees and powder
Are something else

# 25

# January 29, 2022

Living in the cold mountains
Doing various activities
Riding through the snow
Listening to the wind blow

It's fun, but it makes you tired
But it's a good tired
The type of feeling
Where you know you're doing
Things you like and enjoy
And fatigue is just the byproduct

Like a heavy, warm blanket
This worn-out feeling
Drapes itself over me

But I don't mind
As I sit and drift

## 26

# January 29, 2022

The mysterious wind
Blows in the night
Outside temp of four degrees

Inside the sturdy house
I appreciate my shelter
That blocks the weather
And keeps me warm

Winter is here
And matured, and ripened
Below zero is normal
The ice cold is routine

Only the lowest temps
Bite in the early morning hours
Because zero feels
Like a regular day

# 27

# January 31, 2022

Cold, crisp, bright white snow
Gusts of wind blow hard
As I strap on my bindings

Edges cut into ice
Slicing arcs into the slope
Deep scraping sounds
Follow me as I glide
Gaining speed

Green mountain vistas
Make an amphitheater
Amplifying the moments

I make turns – big, small, medium
Taking in the joy
Of the experience

## 28

# January 31, 2022

Freshly woken up
Bowl of oatmeal with milk and honey
I drink two cups of coffee
As the natural light
Bathes me with energy

Trees reach into the sky
Seeking rays of the sun
Their unique outlines
Highlighted against the atmosphere

Stillness and quiet
Permeate the surroundings
As the world comes to life
For another day
In the Green Mountains

# 29

# February 3, 2022

The first storm is here
Yes, there was some snow earlier
But not like this

During the day, rain changed
To sleet and then snow
And now it softly falls in waves
As night sets in
Layer upon layer of crystals
Fall one on top of the other
Atop the Green Mountains
Atop Mt. Mansfield

I feel anticipation
And excitement
My snowboard is ready
Along with other things
I will go to bed soon
And await tomorrow

# 30

# February 4, 2022

The alarm went off at 4:00 am
I was eager to ride the fresh powder
With around 10 inches of new snow
Blanketing the slopes of Stowe Mountain Resort
I could barely wait to hit the road

After oatmeal and coffee
I carefully got my equipment ready
And walked outside into the
Changed landscape
With my car near the driveway's end
I shoveled away some snow in its path
Then nosed onto the road
And began the journey

Every move of the steering wheel
I made with caution
As the driving snow
Pelted the windshield

But I kept at it, just kept driving
At a steady pace
Paying attention to the traction
And keeping my speed low

About 10 miles from the mountain
The outside world
Looked like an arctic moonscape
Everything covered in white

During some moments,
I wondered if I'd make it
To the mountain

Finally, I reached the lift line
And began a long day of riding
It was 8:00 a.m.

On my fish snowboard
I explored the forests
And glided, and glided
Time after time
Through pillowy crystals

Even as more tracks appeared
In the forest
I kept searching and finding
New lines and pockets of powder

Whipping and slashing my board

Finessing it around corners
And threading through trees
The glades became a
Snowy obstacle course

As the day went on
I wore down
I took breaks
But I couldn't stop riding
The snow was too good

Just one more lap
Just one more lift ride
Another trip through the glades
In search of more soft powder
So I can feel it under my feet again

This kept up all day long
Until finally the clock read 4:00 p.m.
The lifts were closed

It felt good to take advantage
Of the wonderful conditions

The ride home was as treacherous
As in the morning, if not more so
But finally, I reached the warm
House on a hill, the outside light
Like of beacon of warmth and safety

Inside, warm food and comfort

Thawed my system
From an ideal powder day
At Stowe Mountain Resort

31

# February 5, 2022

It's the morning after
An 8:00 to 4:00 powder day
I'm worn down and weak
But it feels good

It feels good knowing I spent all day
Floating through the snow
Dodging between the trees
Taking a different line each time
And getting the most out of the day

Today, I will rest and recover
Let the natural light bathe me
As it glows through the windows

The snow-covered trees outside
Serving as a reminder
Of yesterday
And how much fun I had

# 32

# February 5, 2022

Post-snowstorm and
Vermont radiates winter energy
Blankets and speckles of white
Cover the landscape

All the powdery crystals
Absorbing sounds
Creating a still atmosphere
Nature functioning
Like a well-oiled machine

Various creatures
Going about their day
Content to exist
And feed on the forest

I listen to the hum
Of the refrigerator
As I take it all in

# 33

## February 8, 2022

It was a little warmer on the mountain today
I got hot at times and had to unzip my jacket
And let the breeze cool me down
I taught a 7-year-old girl to snowboard
All day long, from about 9:00 to 3:00 or so
And I am so, so tired now
But it feels good

Seeing the joy on her face
And the thrill she had sliding on the snow
Stayed with me long after I drove back
I sit here now, warming up on the couch

And I can remember her smile
As she got accustomed
To new sensations and feelings
Over and over again, down the hill
Not wanting to stop, showing
Her parents what she could do

# 34

# February 8, 2022

The drive home from Stowe Mountain Resort
Takes about an hour
I take the winding roads of Rt. 108
And Rt. 100, passing by eclectic places
And taking in the Vermont winter

Then, it's on to I-89 and the long,
Meandering highway that
Wears you out with its drawn-out
Turns and stretches

Exit 8 takes me into the heart of Montpelier
Where I navigate into and out of town
Then heading to the rustic hills
Of Worcester and the mountain house
Where I reside

For some reason, one hour feels like 30 minutes
Maybe it's because I enjoy the ride

35

# February 9, 2022

The day began on the mountain hopefully
I thought I'd get some extra time
To snowboard on my own, relax a little, teach a little
But then I was told, go this way, you have a student
Momentary freedom gone, I trudged to
The snowboard lesson area

I then discovered my 7-year-old girl student
From the previous day had returned

With a mixture of gladness and disappointment
I began teaching her, still tired from yesterday
But as minutes and hours passed by, something happened
Her careful movements and falls
Turned into s-shaped turns down the hill
She became a snowboarder

In between talking about pizza
And which mountain she'd like to

Shred down on her board
She practiced and practiced
And I was elated to see her progress

Today's experience made me reflect
On whether some things
Are more important than others

Although satisfying yourself
May feel good
It isn't much compared to helping
Someone out and improving
Their life in some way

My little 7-year-old friend
Now knows a sport
That she can participate in
For the rest of her time on the planet

It's my hope she keeps snowboarding
More and more, making discovery after discovery
But whatever happens,
We had a great two days together
Practicing, learning, and having fun

# February 10, 2022

Today was somewhat of a break
From punishing cold
And stiff, arctic winds

Temperatures in the mid-30s
And sunny skies
Felt like late spring in a way

As the afternoon waned
And the golden sun shined
Through the windows
I felt calm and renewed
If only for a moment

A healthy dinner warmed me up
Then I sat by the lamp
And read various things

37

# February 12, 2022

Here and there
I notice little hints of spring
Early in the morning, when I leave Worcester
For Stowe Mountain Resort
It's under the soft light of dawn

And when I return to the house
After a long day of snowboarding
And instructing
The same gentle light leads the way
Some days reach into the 40s
Although rarely does that happen
Tomorrow morning is back to single digits
With highs in the teens

Still, you can feel less of a bite
When you step outside
Though winter remains
At a mature level

# 38

# February 12, 2022

With so much back and forth
To Stowe four days per week
Along with other responsibilities
Oftentimes, it feels like there's no time
To stop, rest, and relax

But it's in those seldom moments
Where I savor the pause
Bathed in natural light
From the large windows on the house
Watching snowflakes scatter in the air
And take in what Vermont's all about

In Vermont, I feel tucked away
From the high-paced, stressful
Aspects of daily living
Free to exist as though
In a simpler time or a different era

**39**

**February 16, 2022**

As a boy, I enjoyed small spaces
Like making a fort in the woods
Or crawling under a heap of blankets
Maybe that's why I like Hunger Mountain Co-op

Big box grocery stores' scale is too much
With tall ceilings and bright lights
I feel lost and concerned

But at Hunger Mountain, I feel safe and secure
Browsing the tiny aisles
Row after row of eclectic foods
Like how it used to be in the old days
Where people shopped at small grocery stores
And paid in cash

Each item I buy feels special
Whether cheese, eggs, bread, milk or coffee
It all feels like artisan quality goods

45

And yes, it does cost more
Maybe a good bit more than a supermarket
But it's worth it and I love it
And enjoy supporting a small business

# February 16, 2022

Sometimes, I find myself dreaming
About childhood and simpler times
Gas stations on the corner
Little stores here and there

The times before giant retailers
And strip mall after strip mall
When there was more heart to the surroundings
And less computerized capitalism

Maybe that's why I like Vermont
Here, I feel taken back
When I drive through the country
And see old buildings and businesses
And feel the history of a place
Resistant to some aspects
Of the modern world

Green mountains in the distance
And country roads up ahead
Vermont makes simple life
Real again

# 41

## February 17, 2022

Like any snowboarder
I hope for big snowfalls and powder days
But unfortunately, a lull has arrived in the VT winter
Temperatures in the 40s were bad enough
But today they'll reach the 50s, along with rain

As I look out the window, steady showers fall
Regular in their cadence like a pendulum
Or an old clock
Maybe it's okay though
The rain is a respite of sorts, like a day off
From the winter cold and snow
That challenges you day after day
It's my hope true winter weather returns

Along with good snowfalls
And deep powder in the Stowe trees
For now, I'll wait, and take in the peaceful precipitation
As I rest for a few days away from the mountain

# 42

# February 18, 2022

Outside the window
Snow falls like tiny feathers
Sometimes whipped up by the wind
And whirled around
As if inside a snow globe

With yesterday's rain now passed
I hope winter emerges again
The tornado of flakes outside
Seem to indicate that it might

These flakes this morning
Are so unique
Rather than falling straight down
They float, rise, and fall
Seemingly looking for a good path

They're almost like a flock of birds
Flying this way and that
As they match the direction
Of the wind

# 43

## February 19, 2022

For the moment, winter is back
Snow falls outside the window
Like weightless coconut flakes

As the Vermont countryside
Becomes whiter and whiter
It comes into its own
Like fruit reaching ripeness
Or the moments around sunset

Snow makes Vermont even sweeter
The trees stand tall
Their branches increasingly weighed down
By layers of white
As the tally grows
Flake by flake

I'm inside the house
Where it's warm and quiet
With only the sound of the heat
Through the vents
As I watch the day unfold

# 44

## February 21, 2022

This morning, gray skies, almost white
We have a week of up and down weather ahead
Rain and warm weather Tuesday and Wednesday
Followed by a snowstorm Friday

Some call this period "False Spring"
And I hope they're correct
Still, despite less than ideal weather
I take pleasure in teaching snowboarding

Forming a bond with a student
Letting them know you're their advocate
And helping them progress
Leaves me with satisfaction and contentment

Whether family members learning together
Or children struggling to turn
Each person needs something different
I'm looking forward to Friday's snow

And the Vermont landscape
Once again covered in a blanket of white

# 45

## February 23, 2022

After days and weeks of varied weather
Stormy, snowy days are set to return
As I left the mountain today, strong squalls formed
Transforming the landscape back to its winter shades

On Friday, around a foot is set to fall
And now, two days prior, you can feel it
In the air, as skies turn gray and
Cold winds whip up dust and ice crystals

There's a stillness, almost like the trough of a wave
Creating a void for energy to occupy
And just like a wave crests and crashes
A storm rolls in and releases moisture

I look forward to watching the flakes
Softly fall outside the windows
And the forest go even quieter
As winter returns to Vermont

# 46

## February 24, 2022

The day before the storm
As the sun rises over the treeline
Tinges of spring's sweetness fill the air
Golden yellow light illuminates
The tips of branches as the world awakes

The treetops form an outline
Against the blue sky
Offering no hints of impending snow

Splotches of white intermingle
With tree trunks, rivers, and rocks
In need of replenishment
Before winter dries up

Today's changeover will be interesting
As winter regains its grasp
Over the surroundings
And the Vermont snow globe returns

# 47

# February 24, 2022 (evening)

As the sun set over the blue skies
And the snowstorm grew closer
I ran along the river

Sweet, pure, fresh air
Like I've never tasted
Whipped up by the cold currents
As they wound underneath ice and rocks

The soft, muddy roads of yesterday were now frozen
After the cold arrived today
Signaling winter's return
Despite being worn out from snowboarding
I enjoyed striding and jumping
Down the road, free for the moment
Only me and nature
And the river making ideal sounds

## 48

# February 25, 2022

Snow steadily falls in quiet waves
Not floating or tumbling
Or whipping in the wind
Just a constant stream
The way a river flows

I'm wondering how much will fall
And how long it will last
Now, around 8:30 am, I can't tell

The skies are opaque gray
And chalky, and white
Full of moisture ready to drop down

Inside the house, it's warm and quiet
The refrigerator hums
Golden lights glow
And I observe the snow
As the day unfolds

# 49

## February 25, 2022 (afternoon)

Around 3:00 pm, flakes continue to fall
Like little down feathers
They evenly float to the earth

Everything feels so soft
Peace and quiet all around
Tomorrow, I intend to wake up early
In search of powder runs
Flowing through the trees
Time after time
Under blue skies and bright sun

For now, I will enjoy the storm's remainder
Eat warm food and sit by the lamp
Awaiting what tomorrow brings
Until I set out for the mountain

# 50

# February 26, 2022

Tasting powder between Stowe's trees
All morning long
Special snow like powdery ice cream
The sun peeking over the mountains
Outlines of bark against the sky

I harvested as many soft puffs
Of snow under my board
As I could, and wandered all around
Until my energy ran dry

Every trip through the trees is different
Tracks here and there
And leftover snow off to the side
Riding powder is a special feeling
Gliding and floating, and
Being in touch with nature

# 51

## March 2, 2022

Stowe is a soul mountain
When you duck inside the trees
Off of Toll Road, you enter a secret spot

Quiet and undiscovered
Mound after mound of thick snow
Waiting for you to plow and glide

As more tracks appear
You become a snow hunter
Weaving around and under
Trees, branches, undulations

When you see more snow
It's a matter of finding a way there
And dodging right and left
So you can feel that sweet slide
One more time

And make more turns
Kicking up snow like white
Glittery dust.

52

# March 3, 2022


Early March in Vermont
Winter lingers and flakes continue to fall
But the sunlight is sweeter
And slightly warmer temps ease the
Burden of the biting cold

This morning, large flakes
Float to the ground outside
And there's a faint blue hue
To the light

The weather continues to be
Up and down, mild then cold
So I cherish the mornings
Where snow's plentiful,
Signifying winter's continuation

I know the season ends this month
And I have mixed feelings about it
But for now, I sit in the morning glow
And take in Vermont's winter beauty

53

# March 3, 2022

The sun glows through the window
Outside the house, the wind gusts
And kicks up snow
I can feel winter wane, degree by degree
Yet it still remains and
Snow covers the ground and the forest

Branches blow in the wind
Partially covered by the fading light
As the sun slowly sinks
Further and further
Until the cold takes over

The house keeps me warm
As I take a rest day
Before heading to the mountain
For snowboarding and sunlight

# 54

# March 5, 2022

The sun wanes through the window
After a day at the house
Taking care of various things

I'm worn down from driving
Back to the mountain again and again
And from snowboarding
But that doesn't mean I want to stop

Snow's fallen again and again
Over the past week or so
And the mountain's in great condition
But tomorrow, rain arrives for the day

I hope the snow holds up
Until the week begins and possibly
More flakes fall

It's a little mild today, 35 or so
Easier on the senses
But I still await colder temps
Before next month is here

# 55

## March 6, 2022

After a sweet few weeks of winter
Today, the rain arrived
Heavy, pouring rain at Stowe
Then temps in the 50s later on

It was disappointing
But as spring draws closer
I just had to roll with it

The snow was sticky
My board tried to glide
But at times barely could
I did some teaching
And made it through the day
As tinges of spring sunlight
Fell over the green mountains

The rest of the week is supposed to be cooler
So I hope winter stays a little longer

# March 8, 2022

After a discouraging respite
Winter is poking through again
Overnight, rain turned to snow
And now, outside the windows
Flurries circulate in the air
As the wind gusts back and forth

Flakes happily float to the ground
Under a gray sky
The air is still inside the house
As I prepare to visit the mountain
I'm unsure how the conditions will be
But simply look forward to being there

Less than two weeks left
In the season, yet it hangs on
Nature thriving and functioning
As it has throughout time

# 57

# March 8, 2022

Today, all sorts of forces
Were on Mount Mansfield
Driving wind, pelting snow, glowing sun
Like its own little private climate

I rode from around 9:00 a.m. to 2:00 p.m.
The snow was so good at first
But as time passed, ice appeared
And my board slipped on the slopes

Still, there were pockets of good snow
Here and there, as the wind kept
Blowing and blowing below
The bright sun

The afternoon light gave hints of spring
Yet the temps were still those of winter

# 58

# March 8, 2022

After an off-and-on winter of
Warm temps and icy slopes
A storm arrives on Saturday

Predictions range from 12 to 21 inches
And could refresh the piste
And extend the season

Besides that, the possibility
Of gliding through the
Ice cream-like powder at Stowe
Fills me with anticipation

Tree runs, powder mists, and more
Under sunny skies would be sweet
For now, temps are back to winter ones
20s right now, as the sun rises
And I wait for the weekend

# 59

# March 11, 2022

This evening, a storm slowly approaches
Bringing the possibility of over a foot of snowfall
This season, the weather's been all over the map
Making a big snow even more special

The afternoon sky was gray
The way it tends to be before a storm
Overnight, the snow should begin
Then fall all day, into the evening
And maybe overnight into Sunday

I wonder what it will be like
How strong the snowfall will be
And how quickly it adds up
But snow is a treat
No matter how much or how little

# 60

## March 12, 2022

The storm is here
As the sun rises, hidden behind a gray sky
Flakes fall urgently to the ground

The snow doesn't float or meander in the air
It drives downward
As if it has important work to do

Layer upon layer of unique crystals
Build up slowly but surely
As the storm takes shape
And the environment slowly changes

The air is still
The surrounding forests
Absorbing the flakes
As winter reappears

# 61

# March 14, 2022

With about a week in the season left
Winter hangs on
After a weekend storm and bountiful powder
This morning, a gray sky offers even more

Whimsical flakes flutter and drop
For a light, peaceful coating
The forest looks as it always has

It has been a long winter
With ups and downs
Cold and warm days
Deep powder and ice and cord

But the good conditions
Make up for the poor ones
And feeling the glide of fresh snow
Has been special

62

March 18, 2022

It was balmy on the mountain today
Slush, soft snow, sunlight, clouds
I sprayed waves of snow with my board
As I felt winter fading

Bare spots appeared on the trails
Only days after a winter storm
The constant warmth and rain
Just too much

I'm hopeful for cold weather and snow
To finish out the snowboard season
But as winter ends
I have mixed emotions

Teaching snowboarding can be wonderful
But also tiring, wearing you down

In a way, I look forward to easier days
Under the sun
As spring arrives and
Thaws the surroundings

## March 20, 2022

It's before dawn
The last minutes and hours of winter
Slowly go by, holding on until
Spring finally arrives this morning

Winter 21/22 had many variations
Snowstorms, rain, subzero mornings
And Mt. Mansfield was like
Its own little world through it all

I will miss many things about the season
But it's been a grind, with much driving
Back and forth to snowboard and teach
With not much time to stop and rest

Winter in Vermont is special
Bitter, arctic, punishing, yet sweet
Experiencing it has been a pleasure
I now wait until next year